Management Accounting: Budgeting

Workbook

Aubrey Penning

Published by Osborne Books Limited
Tel 01905 748071
Email books@osbornebooks.co.uk
Website www.osbornebooks.co.uk

Design by Laura Ingham

Printed by CPI Group (UK) Limited, Croydon, CR0 4YY, on environmentally friendly, acid-free paper from managed forests.

British Library Cataloguing in Publication Data
A catalogue record for this book is available from the British Library

ISBN 978 1909173 903

Contents

Introduction

Chapter activities

Answers to chapter activities

Practice assessments

Answers to practice assessments

Also available from Osborne Books...

Tutorials

Clear, explanatory books written
precisely to the specifications

Student Zone

Login to access your free ebooks and
interactive revision crosswords

Download **Osborne Books App** free from the App Store or Google Play Store
to view your ebooks online or offline on your mobile or tablet.

www.osbornebooks.co.uk

Introduction

Qualifications covered

This book has been written specifically to cover the Unit 'Management Accounting: Budgeting' which is mandatory for the following qualifications:

■ AAT Professional Diploma in Accounting – Level 4

■ AAT Professional Diploma in Accounting at SCQF – Level 8

This book contains Chapter Activities which provide extra practice material in addition to the activities included in the Osborne Books Tutorial text, and Practice Assessments to prepare the student for the computer based assessments. The latter are based directly on the structure, style and content of the sample assessment material provided by the AAT at www.aat.org.uk.

Suggested answers to the Chapter Activities and Practice Assessments are set out in this book.

Osborne Study and Revision Materials

The materials featured on the previous page are tailored to the needs of students studying this Unit and revising for the assessment. They include:

■ **Tutorials:** paperback books with practice activities

■ **Student Zone:** access to Osborne Books online resources

■ **Osborne Books App:** Osborne Books ebooks for mobiles and tablets

Visit www.osbornebooks.co.uk for details of study and revision resources and access to online material.

Chapter activities

1   Management accounting techniques

1.1   A manufacturing company which makes a single product has the following annual budgeted costs:

	£
Direct materials	190,000
Direct labour	160,000
Fixed production overheads	480,000
Fixed non-production overheads	150,000

The normal budgeted production per year is 60,000 units. Direct materials and direct labour costs behave as variable costs.

Select the correct absorption cost per unit and marginal cost per unit from the following lists, which are both calculated to the nearest penny.

Absorption cost per unit		Marginal cost per unit	
(a) £8.00		(a) £8.33	
(b) £16.33		(b) £5.83	
(c) £13.83		(c) £3.17	
(d) £5.67		(d) £10.50	

1.2   Select an appropriate accounting system to deal with each of the following situations:

(a)	Manufacturing production process with high overheads and set-up costs	
(b)	Labour intensive manufacturing industry	
(c)	Budgeting for a manufacturing organisation where future output level is very uncertain	
(d)	Machine intensive production process with known output levels and long production runs	

Options:

1   Absorption costing using labour hours to absorb overheads

2   Marginal costing

3   Activity based costing

4   Absorption costing using machine hours to absorb overheads

1.3 Calculate the appropriate budgeted overhead recovery rate for the following Production Department. The department's annual budget for indirect costs is:

	£
Indirect labour	38,500
Supervisor wages	19,500
Depreciation of equipment	4,000
Machine maintenance	6,780
Canteen subsidy	11,220
Total	**80,000**

Notes: The budget production of 3,000 units will require 8,000 machine hours and 40,000 direct labour hours.

Complete the following:

Overhead recovery should be based on **Labour hours / Machine hours**.

The recovery rate will be [   ] per [   ] .

1.4 Calculate the appropriate budgeted overhead recovery rate for the following Production Department. The department's annual budget for indirect costs is:

	£
Indirect labour	18,000
Supervisor wages	21,900
Depreciation of equipment	35,000
Machine maintenance	23,500
Canteen subsidy	3,600
Total	**102,000**

Notes: The budget production of 5,000 units will require 12,750 machine hours and 1,020 direct labour hours.

Complete the following:

Overhead recovery should be based on **Labour hours / Machine hours.**

The recovery rate will be [   ] per [   ] .

1.5 A company wishes to estimate how its overheads behave when production volumes change.

(a) Complete the following table, and by using the high-low method calculate the expected variable costs (per unit) and fixed costs (per month).

	Cost per month £	Output per month *(units)*
Data provided	70,000	10,000
Data provided	90,000	14,000
Difference		
Variable cost per unit		
Fixed cost per month		

(b) Using the information calculated in part (a), complete the following table to show the breakdown of estimated costs at a monthly production level of 13,500 units.

	£
Variable costs	
Fixed costs	
Total costs	

2 Forecasting techniques

2.1 Match the data in the first column with the appropriate source selected from the second column.

Data
Social trends in UK
Views of prospective customers
Current material costs
Competitors' performance

Source
Production schedule
Office for National Statistics
Market research
SWOT analysis
HMRC website
Financial press
Suppliers' quotations

2.2 This year's sales are £1,500,000. Analysis of recent years shows:

- a growth trend of 3% per annum
- seasonal variations from the trend of:

Quarter 1	−£50,000
Quarter 2	+£10,000
Quarter 3	+£75,000
Quarter 4	−£35,000

Forecast the sales for each quarter of next year, using the following table.

	£
Quarter 1	
Quarter 2	
Quarter 3	
Quarter 4	
Total Sales	

2.3   Next year's sales were originally forecast at £5,414,850, assuming a 5% selling price increase from this year. The increase has now been agreed at 3% instead. Assuming the sales volume does not alter from the original forecast, calculate the revised sales forecast.

(a) £5,306,553	
(b) £5,311,710	
(c) £5,577,296	
(d) £5,253,405	

2.4   Electricity costs for the last year were £240,000, based on a price of 10p per kWh used. The forecast for next year shows a reduction in consumption of 5% due to energy saving measures, but a price increase of 8%. Using the following table, calculate the electricity budget for next year. Do not round any figures.

Current year's usage (kWh)	
Next year's usage (kWh)	
Current year's price per kWh (£)	
Next year's price per kWh (£)	
Budget for electricity next year (£)	

2.5 The budget for the cost of gas for next year was originally set at £121,000. This assumed a 10% increase in costs from last year, and assumed that consumption would not change.

It is now believed that the unit cost will increase by 7% from last year, but that consumption will increase by 4%.

Complete the following:

The cost of gas last year was £ [　　　　　] .

Allowing for both a change in consumption and a price increase, the budget for next year should be £ [　　　　　] .

2.6 The trend in the number of units sold per quarter was 7,400 in the last quarter of the current year. The trend increases by 50 units per quarter.

The seasonal variations are a percentage of the trend for the quarter, and have been established as:

Quarter 1	−10%
Quarter 2	−15%
Quarter 3	+35%
Quarter 4	−10%

The selling price for each unit will be £22 in the next year. Complete the following table to establish the data for the sales budget for next year. Calculate the unit forecast to the nearest whole unit.

	Trend *(units)*	Forecast *(units)*	Forecast sales £
Quarter 1			
Quarter 2			
Quarter 3			
Quarter 4			
Totals			

3 Functional budgets

3.1 Complete the following table by using ticks to show into which budget each item of cost would occur.

	Cost of production	Maintenance	Capital expenditure	Marketing	Finance
Direct labour wages					
Interest charges					
New computer system					
Entertaining customers					
Hire of machinery testing equipment					
Raw materials usage					

3.2 Complete the following table to show the forecast inventories and production units for a particular product.

Closing inventory should be 40% of the following week's forecast sales.

Number of Units	Week 1	Week 2	Week 3	Week 4	Week 5
Opening inventory	4,000				
Production					
Sub-total					
Forecast sales	10,000	12,500	11,000	10,500	12,000
Closing inventory					

Forecast sales in week 6 are 10,000 units.

3.3   24,000 units of finished product are to be manufactured during October. Each unit takes four minutes to produce. Nine staff each work 160 basic hours in October.

The number of overtime hours required to be worked in October is [   ] .

3.4   Department K manufactures three products, Alpha, Beta and Gamma.

Calculate the machine hours required to manufacture these in November, using the following table.

Product	Units	Hours per unit	Hours required
Alpha	190	1.0	
Beta	200	2.5	
Gamma	270	3.2	
Total machine hours for department K			

There are three machines in the department.

Each machine can be used for 350 hours in November. Additional machines can be hired if required.

How many additional machines should be hired? [   ]

3.5   The number of units of a product that are required are shown below. 5% of the units produced fail a quality control test and are scrapped. Complete the table to show the number of units that must be manufactured to allow for this rejection rate.

	Month 1	Month 2	Month 3
Required units	76,000	77,900	81,700
Manufactured units			

3.6   19,000 units of finished product are to be manufactured in September. Each finished unit contains 3 kg of raw material. 5% of the raw material input is wasted during production. Inventories of raw material are to be:

- opening inventory   30,000 kg

- closing inventory   25,000 kg

Select the quantity of raw material to be purchased from the following:

(a) 55,000 kg	
(b) 57,000 kg	
(c) 54,850 kg	
(d) 49,150 kg	

4   Master budgets

4.1   From the following list, identify those responsibilities which may typically be part of the role of the budget accountant.

(a) Authorise all capital expenditure	
(b) Ensure that all budgets are fully coordinated	
(c) Monitor budgets against actual performance and prepare reports on significant variances	
(d) Submit company tax returns to HMRC	
(e) Ensure that the budget timetable is followed by all participants	
(f) Advise and assist functional managers in their budget submissions	

4.2 The following production budget for a month has been prepared.

Production budget	Units
Opening inventory of finished goods	5,000
Production	40,000
Sub-total	45,000
Sales	38,000
Closing inventory of finished goods	7,000

(a) Complete the following working schedule for raw materials. Each unit produced requires 0.75 kg of material. Closing inventory is valued at budgeted purchase price.

Raw materials	kg	£
Opening inventory of raw materials	3,500	7,000
Purchases of raw materials	32,000	64,000
Sub-total	35,500	71,000
Used in production		
Closing inventory of raw materials		

(b) Complete the following working schedule for direct labour. Each unit takes six minutes to make. There are 22 direct labour employees, each working 160 basic hours in the month. Additional hours are paid at an overtime rate of time and a half. The overtime premium is included in the direct labour cost.

Direct labour	Hours	Cost £
Basic time at £10 per hour		
Overtime		
Total		

(c) Complete the following working schedule for overheads. Variable overheads are recovered based on total labour hours worked.

Overheads	Hours	Cost £
Variable overheads at £2.00 per hour		
Fixed overheads		12,000
Total overheads		

(d) Complete the following operating budget, using information from the earlier tasks. Closing inventory of finished goods is to be valued at budgeted production cost per unit.

Operating budget	Units	per unit £	£
Sales		4.50	
Cost of goods sold:			
Opening inventory of finished goods			15,300
Cost of production:		£	
Raw Materials			
Direct labour			
Production overheads			
Total cost of production			
Closing inventory of finished goods			
Cost of goods sold			
Gross profit			
Non-production overheads		£	
Administration		15,000	
Marketing		12,500	
Total non-production overheads			
Net profit			

4.3 The following budget data has been prepared.

Budget data	June £	July £	August £	Sept £
Credit sales	8,900	8,300	8,800	9,500
Purchases	4,200	5,100	4,800	4,900
Wages	2,300	2,350	2,300	2,400
Expenses	1,050	1,080	1,070	1,090
Capital expenditure	2,000		4,500	

Timings:

60% of credit sales are received in the month after sale, the remainder one month later.

Purchases are paid in the month after purchase.

Wages are paid in the month incurred.

Expenses are paid in the month after they are incurred. Expenses include £200 per month depreciation.

Capital expenditure is paid immediately as it is incurred.

Complete a cash forecast for August, using the following table.

Cash forecast – August	£
Opening cash balance	16,400
Receipts from sales	
Payments for:	
Purchases	
Wages	
Expenses	
Capital expenditure	
Total payments	
Closing cash balance	

4.4   You have prepared a draft budget for direct material costs.

·   It is based on the current usage of material per unit produced, together with the current cost per kilo plus an expected cost increase.

·   The Purchasing Manager has forecast the cost increase.

·   You have calculated the total required material usage from the agreed production budget.

·   You understand that there are no planned changes to raw material inventory levels.

·   You have been asked to suggest appropriate performance measures that would assist managers to monitor direct material costs against budget.

Direct material budget

	This year	Next year's budget
Production units	430,000	500,000
Raw materials per unit (kg)	0.35	0.35
Total raw material usage (kg)	150,500	175,000
Cost of raw materials used (£)	£1,053,500	£1,261,750

Write an email to the Production Director:

(a)   Explaining the calculations and assumptions and requesting his approval.

(b)   Suggesting appropriate direct material performance indicators for this department.

Email

To:

From:

Date:

Subject:

5 Revising budgets

5.1 The following information is available about a company that makes a single product.

- Each unit is made from 1.5 kg of material costing £1.80 per kg.

- It takes 15 minutes to make each item.

- 800 hours of basic labour time is available in the month of April. Any extra hours must be worked in overtime.

- The basic labour rate is £12 per hour. Overtime is paid at time and a half (50% more than basic rate).

- Variable overhead relates to labour hours worked, including overtime.

- Fixed overhead costs are incurred evenly through the year.

Complete the following table with the April budget figures.

	Budget for the year	Budget for April
Units sold	36,000	3,000
Units produced	40,000	3,500
	£	£
Sales	540,000	
Cost of production:		
Materials used	108,000	
Labour	122,400	
Variable production overhead	20,000	
Fixed production overhead	18,000	

5.2   Calculate the sales budget, and the budgets that make up the cost of production for week 14.

	Budget for the year	Budget for week 14
Units sold	850,000	16,800
Units produced	860,000	17,000
	£	£
Sales	8,075,000	
Costs of production:		
Materials used	1,754,400	
Labour	2,720,000	
Variable production overhead	1,978,000	
Fixed production overhead	1,040,000	
Total cost of production	7,492,400	

Each unit is made from 1.7 litres of material costing £1.20 per litre.

It takes 12 minutes to make each unit. There are 3,000 labour hours available each week at basic rate of £15.00 per hour. Any hours required over this are paid at an overtime rate of £20.00 per hour.

Fixed production overhead accrues evenly over the year.

5.3   Machine hire is a stepped fixed cost for a particular organisation. Each machine can produce up to 13,000 units in a year. The cost of supervision is budgeted at £45,000 when annual output is 70,000 units.

Calculate the budgeted cost of supervision for annual unit production of:

(a)   60,000 units

(b)   68,000 units

(c)   80,000 units

5.4 A company has already produced budgets based on its first scenario.

Assumptions in the first scenario:

- Materials and labour are variable costs
- Depreciation is a stepped fixed cost increasing every 15,000 units
- Energy costs is semi-variable, with a fixed element of £48,000
- Occupancy costs behave as fixed costs

The alternative scenario is based on:

- An increase in selling price of 2%
- A decrease in sales volume of 5%
- An increase in only the variable cost of energy of 3%
- An increase in occupancy costs of 2.5%

Apart from the selling price per unit, do not enter any decimals. Round to the nearest whole number if necessary.

Operating budget	First scenario	Alternative scenario
Selling price per unit	£11.50	
Sales volume	190,000	
	£	£
Sales revenue	2,185,000	
Costs:		
Materials	541,500	
Labour	570,000	
Depreciation	182,000	
Energy	124,000	
Occupancy costs	203,600	
Total costs	1,621,100	
Operating profit	563,900	
Increase / (decrease) in profit		

Complete the alternative scenario column in the operating budget table and calculate the increase or decrease in expected profit.

5.5 A company has already completed the following operating budget for the manufacture and sale of two products during the month of July.

Operating budget July	Product Xenox	Product Zenley	Total
Manufacture & sales volume	30,000	50,000	80,000
	£	£	£
Sales revenue	360,000	900,000	1,260,000
Variable costs:			
Materials	90,000	120,000	210,000
Labour	120,000	350,000	470,000
Contribution	150,000	430,000	580,000
Fixed costs			450,000
Operating profit			130,000

Both products use the same material, which costs £0.60 per kilo.

It has now been established that the amount of material available for July production will be limited to 250,000 kilos.

Required:

(a) Calculate the revised volume of manufacture and sale of each product in July that will maximise the operating profit from the available resources.

(b) Complete a revised operating budget for July, using the following table, based on your solution to part **(a)**.

Revised operating budget July	Product Xenox	Product Zenley	Total
Manufacture & sales volume			
	£	£	£
Sales revenue			
Variable costs:			
Materials			
Labour			
Contribution			
Fixed costs			
Operating profit			

6 Monitoring and controlling performance with budgets

6.1 The operating statement that forms part of the following table has been produced, using the original fixed budget (based on production and sales of 50,000 units) and the actual costs which occurred when 60,000 units were produced and sold.

Using the data in the operating statement, together with the notes shown below, complete the flexed budget and variances in the appropriate columns in the table.

	Original budget	Actual	Flexed budget	Variances Fav / (Adv)
Volume (units)	50,000	60,000	60,000	
	£	£	£	£
Sales revenue	2,250,000	2,640,000		
Costs:				
Materials	600,000	780,000		
Labour	750,000	895,000		
Distribution	200,000	255,000		
Energy	79,000	85,000		
Equipment hire	15,000	22,000		
Depreciation	24,000	24,000		
Marketing	28,000	30,000		
Administration	45,000	44,500		
Total Costs	1,741,000	2,135,500		
Operating profit	509,000	504,500		

Notes on budget:

- Material, labour and distribution costs are variable.

- The budget for energy is semi-variable. The fixed element is £4,000.

- Equipment hire budget is based on a cost of £3,000 for each 11,000 units or fewer.

- Depreciation, marketing and administration costs are fixed.

6.2 The following operating statement has been prepared using marginal costing and a flexed budget.

Operating statement for November	Budget £	Actual £	Variance £ Fav / (Adv)
Sales revenue	96,000	88,000	(8,000)
Variable costs:			
Materials	32,000	30,000	2,000
Labour	16,000	19,000	(3,000)
Distribution	8,000	8,200	(200)
Power	6,000	5,900	100
Contribution	**34,000**	**24,900**	**(9,100)**
Fixed costs:			
Power	2,500	3,000	(500)
Depreciation	3,500	3,300	200
Marketing	5,000	4,500	500
Administration	6,500	6,500	0
Operating profit	**16,500**	**7,600**	**(8,900)**

The original budget was based on producing and selling 1,500 units. The company actually produced and sold 1,600 units, and the budget was flexed to this volume.

You have also established the following information about the operations:

- the quantity of material used was in line with the output produced

- employees worked overtime to cope with the additional output

- there was a change in both fixed and variable power costs imposed by the power supply company

- some non-current assets were sold for their book value; this was not originally planned

Select from the following statements, those that are consistent with the operating statement and information shown on the previous page and could form part of a report.

(a) The sales revenue variance was caused by the difference between the original budgeted output and the actual output.	
(b) The sales revenue variance was caused by selling at a lower average price than budgeted (£55 instead of £60). This may have helped increase the sales from the original budget.	
(c) The favourable material variance could have been caused by either using fewer materials than planned or by obtaining the materials at a cheaper price, or a combination of these factors.	
(d) Since the quantity of materials used was in line with the output, the material cost variance must have been caused by paying a higher price than budgeted for the materials.	
(e) Since the quantity of materials used was in line with the output, the material cost variance must have been caused by paying a lower price than budgeted for the materials.	
(f) A possible cause of the adverse labour cost variance is the need to use overtime hours, which are probably paid at a higher rate than basic hours.	
(g) The labour cost variance may be entirely caused by the difference between the original budgeted output and the actual (higher) output.	
(h) The changes in the power tariff have resulted in less cost overall for power than was budgeted.	
(i) The changes in the power tariff mean that a greater element of the cost is fixed than budgeted, although the variable element seems to have decreased. Overall the total power cost has increased.	
(j) The depreciation charge is decreased due to the profit on sale of the non-current assets.	
(k) The actual depreciation charge is lower than that budgeted since some non-current assets were sold, and are therefore no longer depreciated.	
(l) The overall operating profit adverse variance is mainly accounted for by the reduction in average selling price compared to budget.	

6.3 Unsure Limited originally produced two budgets, one based on an output of 10,000 units, and one based on an output of 15,000 units. The actual output (production and sales) was 11,500 units.

Complete the following table with a flexed budget and variances based on the flexed budget.

	Budget 1	Budget 2	Actual	Flexed budget	Variances Fav / (Adv)
Units	10,000	15,000	11,500	11,500	
	£	£	£	£	£
Sales	900,000	1,350,000	1,058,000		
Materials	250,000	375,000	299,000		
Labour	350,000	500,000	380,000		
Production overheads	170,000	195,000	190,000		
Administration overheads	60,000	60,000	62,000		
Operating profit	70,000	220,000	127,000		

6.4 The standard cost data for one unit of Gamma is as follows:

Materials   7 kilos at £13.60 per kilo

Labour   15 minutes at £18.00 per hour

During May, 1,890 units of Gamma were produced.

The actual inputs were:

13,400 kilos material costing £181,570

480 hours labour costing £9,120

Required:

- Calculate the flexed budget, actual costs and total variances for materials and labour for May

- Calculate the material price variance, the material usage variance, the labour rate variance and the labour efficiency variance for May

Answers to chapter activities

1 Management accounting techniques

1.1   Absorption costing   (c) £13.83

   Working: (£190,000 + £160,000 + £480,000) / 60,000 = £13.83

   Marginal costing   (b) £5.83

   Working: (£190,000 + £160,000) / 60,000 = £5.83

1.2   **(a)**   3

   (b)   1

   (c)   2

   (d)   4

1.3   Overhead recovery should be based on **Labour hours**.

   The recovery rate will be **£2.00** per **direct labour hour**.

1.4   Overhead recovery should be based on **Machine hours.**

   The recovery rate will be **£8.00** per **machine hour**.

1.5   **(a)**

	Cost per month £	Output per month *(units)*
Data provided	70,000	10,000
Data provided	90,000	14,000
Difference	20,000	4,000
Variable cost per unit	£5.00	
Fixed cost per month	£20,000	

   (b)

	£
Variable costs	67,500
Fixed costs	20,000
Total costs	87,500

2 Forecasting techniques

2.1

Data		Source
Social trends in UK	→	Office for National statistics
Views of prospective customers	→	Market Research
Current material costs	→	Suppliers' quotations
Competitors' performance	→	Financial press

2.2

	£
Quarter 1	336,250
Quarter 2	396,250
Quarter 3	461,250
Quarter 4	351,250
Total Sales	1,545,000

2.3 (b) £5,311,710

2.4

Current year's usage (kWh)	2,400,000
Next year's usage (kWh)	2,280,000
Current year's price per kWh (£)	0.10
Next year's price per kWh (£)	0.108
Budget for electricity next year (£)	246,240

2.5 The cost of gas last year was **£110,000**.

Allowing for both a change in consumption and a price increase, the budget for next year should be **£122,408**.

2.6

	Trend *(units)*	Forecast *(units)*	Forecast sales £
Quarter 1	7,450	6,705	147,510
Quarter 2	7,500	6,375	140,250
Quarter 3	7,550	10,193	224,246
Quarter 4	7,600	6,840	150,480
Total		30,113	662,486

3 Functional budgets

3.1

	Cost of production	Maintenance	Capital expenditure	Marketing	Finance
Direct labour wages	✔				
Interest charges					✔
New computer system			✔		
Entertaining customers				✔	
Hire of machinery testing equipment		✔			
Raw materials usage	✔				

3.2

Number of Units	Week 1	Week 2	Week 3	Week 4	Week 5
Opening inventory	4,000	5,000	4,400	4,200	4,800
Production	11,000	11,900	10,800	11,100	11,200
Sub-total	15,000	16,900	15,200	15,300	16,000
Forecast sales	10,000	12,500	11,000	10,500	12,000
Closing inventory	5,000	4,400	4,200	4,800	4,000

3.3 The number of overtime hours required to be worked in October is **160 hours**

3.4

Product	Units	Hours per unit	Hours required
Alpha	190	1.0	190
Beta	200	2.5	500
Gamma	270	3.2	864
Total machine hours for department K			1,554

2 additional machines should be hired.

3.5

	Month 1	Month 2	Month 3
Required units	76,000	77,900	81,700
Manufactured units	80,000	82,000	86,000

3.6   (a)   55,000 kg

4 Master budgets

4.1 (b), (c), (e) and (f)

4.2 **(a)**

Raw materials	kg	£
Opening inventory of raw materials	3,500	7,000
Purchases of raw materials	32,000	64,000
Sub-total	35,500	71,000
Used in production	30,000	60,000
Closing inventory of raw materials	5,500	11,000

(b)

Direct labour	Hours	Cost £
Basic time at £10 per hour	3,520	35,200
Overtime	480	7,200
Total	4,000	42,400

(c)

Overheads	Hours	Cost £
Variable overheads at £2.00 per hour	4,000	8,000
Fixed overheads		12,000
Total overheads		20,000

(d)

Operating budget	Units	£ per unit	£
Sales	38,000	4.50	171,000
Cost of goods sold:			
Opening inventory of finished goods			15,300
Cost of production:		£	
Raw materials		60,000	
Direct labour		42,400	
Production overheads		20,000	
Total cost of production			122,400
Closing inventory of finished goods			21,420
Cost of goods sold			116,280
Gross profit			54,720
Non-production overheads		£	
Administration		15,000	
Marketing		12,500	
Total non-production overheads			27,500
Net profit			27,220

4.3

Cash forecast – August	£
Opening cash balance	16,400
Receipts from sales	8,540
Payments for:	
Purchases	5,100
Wages	2,300
Expenses	880
Capital expenditure	4,500
Total payments	12,780
Closing cash balance	12,160

4.4 **(a)** and **(b)**

Email
To: Production Director
From: Accounting Technician
Date: xx
Subject: Direct Material Budget

Budget Submission

I enclose the proposed direct material budget for your consideration and approval.

The production budget is based on an increase from the current output of 430,000 units to 500,000 units next year, and this assumption has been used for the direct material budget.

The budget assumes the current usage of raw material per unit produced (0.35 kg per unit) will be maintained. It allows for a cost increase of raw materials of 3% from the current level of £7.00 per kg to £7.21 per kg. This cost increase has been provided by the purchasing manager.

Since there is no planned change in the raw material inventory levels, the quantity of material to be purchased will be the same as the budgeted usage.

Please let me know if you need any further information.

Performance Indicators

There are several possible measures to monitor usage and cost of raw materials. We should monitor on a weekly or monthly basis:

- raw material usage per unit produced
- raw material cost per unit produced
- number of faulty units produced due to raw material quality (if any)

If a standard costing system was to be introduced throughout the company, the direct material variances would also prove invaluable for monitoring performance.

5 **Revising budgets**

5.1

	Budget for the year	Budget for April
Units sold	36,000	3,000
Units produced	40,000	3,500
	£	£
Sales	540,000	45,000
Cost of production:		
Materials used	108,000	9,450
Labour	122,400	10,950
Variable production overhead	20,000	1,750
Fixed production overhead	18,000	1,500

5.2

	Budget for the year	Budget for week 14
Units sold	850,000	16,800
Units produced	860,000	17,000
	£	£
Sales	8,075,000	159,600
Costs of production:		
Materials used	1,754,400	34,680
Labour	2,720,000	53,000
Variable production overhead	1,978,000	39,100
Fixed production overhead	1,040,000	20,000
Total cost of production	7,492,400	146,780

5.3 70,000 / 13,000 = between 5 and 6, so 6 machines will be needed at that level of production. Six machines will be able to cope with between 65,001 and 78,000 units.

Budgeted machine hire cost be £45,000 / 6 = £7,500 per machine.

(a) 60,000 units requires 5 machines, costing £37,500

(b) 68,000 units requires 6 supervisors, costing £45,000

(c) 80,000 units requires 7 machines, costing £52,500

5.4

Operating budget	First scenario	Alternative scenario
Selling price per unit	£11.50	£11.73
Sales volume	190,000	180,500
	£	£
Sales revenue	2,185,000	2,117,265
Costs:		
Materials	541,500	514,425
Labour	570,000	541,500
Depreciation	182,000	182,000
Energy	124,000	122,366
Occupancy costs	203,600	208,690
Total costs	1,621,100	1,568,981
Operating profit	563,900	548,284
Increase / (decrease) in profit		(15,616)

5.5   **(a)**   Calculation of usage of material in original budget:

Xenox   £90,000 / £0.60 = 150,000 kilos   (= 5 kilos per unit)

Zenley   £120,000 / £0.60 = 200,000 kilos   (= 4 kilos per unit)

Contribution per kilo of material:

Xenox   £150,000 / 150,000 kilos   = £1.00 per kilo

Zenley   £430,000 / 200,000 kilos   = £2.15 per kilo

Manufacture and sales should therefore be concentrated first on Zenley, followed by Xenox to use remaining material, as follows.

	Production volume	**Material used (kilos)**
Zenley	50,000	200,000
Xenox	10,000	50,000
		250,000

(b)

Revised Operating Budget **July**	**Product Xenox**	**Product Zenley**	**Total**
Manufacture & sales volume	10,000	50,000	60,000
	£	£	£
Sales revenue	120,000	900,000	1,020,000
Variable costs:			
Materials	30,000	120,000	150,000
Labour	40,000	350,000	390,000
Contribution	50,000	430,000	480,000
Fixed costs			450,000
Operating profit			30,000

Monitoring and controlling performance with budgets

6.1

	Original budget	Actual	Flexed budget	Variances Fav / (Adv)
Volume (units)	50,000	60,000	60,000	
	£	£	£	£
Sales revenue	2,250,000	2,640,000	2,700,000	(60,000)
Costs:				
Materials	600,000	780,000	720,000	(60,000)
Labour	750,000	895,000	900,000	5,000
Distribution	200,000	255,000	240,000	(15,000)
Energy	79,000	85,000	94,000	9,000
Equipment hire	15,000	22,000	18,000	(4,000)
Depreciation	24,000	24,000	24,000	0
Marketing	28,000	30,000	28,000	(2,000)
Administration	45,000	44,500	45,000	500
Total Costs	1,741,000	2,135,500	2,069,000	(66,500)
Operating profit	509,000	504,500	631,000	(126,500)

6.2 The following statements are consistent with the operating statement and information provided and could form part of a report.

(b), (e), (f), (i), (k) and (l)

6.3

	Budget 1	Budget 2	Actual	Flexed budget	Variances Fav / (Adv)
Units	10,000	15,000	11,500	11,500	
	£	£	£	£	£
Sales	900,000	1,350,000	1,058,000	1,035,000	23,000
Materials	250,000	375,000	299,000	287,500	(11,500)
Labour	350,000	500,000	380,000	395,000	15,000
Production overheads	170,000	195,000	190,000	177,500	(12,500)
Administration overheads	60,000	60,000	62,000	60,000	(2,000)
Operating profit	70,000	220,000	127,000	115,000	12,000

Flexed Budget Workings:

Sales   Selling price is £90 per unit x 11,500 units = £1,035,000

Materials   Variable cost of £25 per unit x 11,500 units = £287,500

Labour   Semi-variable cost: use high-low method

Variable (£500,000 – £350,000) / (15,000 – 10,000 units)

= £30 per unit

Fixed = £350,000 – (£30 x 10,000) = £50,000

Production Overheads   Semi-variable cost: use high-low method

Variable (£195,000 – £170,000) / (15,000 – 10,000 units)

= £5 per unit

Fixed = £170,000 – (£5 x 10,000) = £120,000

6.4

	Flexed budget £	Actual £	Variance £
Materials	179,928	181,570	1,642 A
Labour	8,505	9,120	615 A

Material Price Variance:

(13,400 kilos x £13.60) - £181,570   =   £ 670 F

Material Usage Variance:

((7 kilos x 1,890) − 13,400 kilos) x £13.60   =   £2,312 A

         Total material variance   £1,642 A

Labour Rate Variance:

(480 hours x £18.00) - £9,120   =   £ 480 A

Labour Efficiency Variance:

((0.25 hours x 1,890) − 480 hours) x £18.00   =   £ 135 A

         Total labour variance   £ 615 A

Practice assessment 1

Task 1

(a)   Match the data in the first column with the appropriate source selected from the second column.

Data
Typical performance in the trade
National economic growth
Corporation tax rates

Source
SWOT analysis
Supplier price lists
Trade association publications
Market research
HMRC publications
Office for National Statistics

(b)   Who would you contact in each of the following situations?

(a) You want to know details of planned pay rises	
(b) You want details of the sales forecast	
(c) You want details of planned acquisitions of non-current assets	

Select from:

1   Capital expenditure budget working group

2   Production Director

3   Purchasing Manager

4   Sales Director

5   Human Resources Manager

6   Marketing Manager

(c) Complete the following table by using ticks to show into which budget(s) each item of cost would occur.

	Direct cost of production	Production overheads	Capital expenditure	Marketing	Cash
Extension to offices					
Depreciation of production equipment					
Indirect production labour					
Advertising campaign costs					
Hire of production equipment					
Printing customer perceptions questionnaire					

(d) Select an appropriate accounting treatment for each of the following costs from the options available.

(a)	Employers' National Insurance for administration staff	
(b)	Material usage for production	
(c)	Rent of photocopier	
(d)	Cost of the stores department	
(e)	Cost of idle time for production operatives	
(f)	Cost of productive time for production operatives	

Options available are:

1   Activity based charge to production cost centres

2   Allocate to administration overheads

3   Direct cost

4   Allocate to finance overheads

5   Allocate to selling and distribution overheads

6   Allocate to production overheads

(e)   This year's sales are £2,500,000. Analysis of recent years shows:

- a growth trend of 2.5% per annum
- seasonal variations from the trend of:

Quarter 1   −£40,000

Quarter 2   +£20,000

Quarter 3   +£55,000

Quarter 4   −£35,000

Forecast the sales for each quarter of next year, using the following table.

	£
Quarter 1	
Quarter 2	
Quarter 3	
Quarter 4	
Total Sales	

Task 2

(a) Complete the following table to show the forecast inventories and production units for a particular product.

Closing inventory should be 25% of the following week's forecast sales.

Number of Units	Week 1	Week 2	Week 3	Week 4	Week 5
Opening inventory	5,000				
Production					
Sub-total					
Forecast sales	20,000	21,500	21,000	20,500	22,000
Closing inventory					

Forecast sales in week 6 are 25,000 units.

(b) The number of units of a product that are required are shown below. 7% of the units produced fail a quality control test and are scrapped. Complete the table to show the number of units that must be manufactured to allow for this rejection rate.

	Month 1	Month 2	Month 3
Required units	75,330	79,980	77,190
Manufactured units			

(c) The following information is available about the plans for June:

- 23,750 units of finished product are to be manufactured.
- Each unit of finished product contains 4.0 kg of raw material.
- 5% of raw material is wasted during manufacture.
- The opening inventory of raw material is 18,000 kg.
- The closing inventory of raw material is to be 20,000 kg.

The purchases of raw material must be:

(a)	100,000 kg	
(b)	95,000 kg	
(c)	8,250 kg	
(d)	98,000 kg	
(e)	102,000 kg	
(f)	101,750 kg	

(d) 50,000 units of finished product are to be manufactured during October. Each unit takes three minutes to produce. 12 staff each work 180 basic hours in October.

Complete the following sentences:

The number of units that can be made in basic time during October is [ ] .

The number of overtime hours required to be worked in October is [ ] .

(e)   A company has budgeted to make and sell 60,000 units in the coming year.

Each unit takes 20 minutes to make and requires 2.5 kg of raw material. The quality control department can test 4,200 units each month. A contract has been placed to purchase 100,000 kg of raw material at an agreed price. Further supplies can be obtained on the open market but the price is likely to be much higher. The company employs 10 production workers. Each worker works 1,750 hours a year in normal time.

Complete the following analysis.

There is labour available to make ⬚ units in normal time. Therefore, ⬚ hours of overtime will be needed.

The raw material contract will provide enough material to make ⬚ units.

Therefore, ⬚ kg will have to be purchased on the open market.

Quality control can test ⬚ units in the year. It will be necessary to make alternative arrangements for ⬚ units.

Task 3

The following production budget for a month has been prepared.

Production budget	Units
Opening inventory of finished goods	3,000
Production	28,000
Sub-total	31,000
Sales	30,000
Closing inventory of finished goods	1,000

(a) Complete the following working schedule for raw materials. Each unit produced requires 1.25 kg of material. Closing inventory is valued at budgeted purchase price.

Raw materials	kg	£
Opening inventory of raw materials	1,800	7,200
Purchases of raw materials	34,000	136,000
Sub-total	35,800	143,200
Used in production		
Closing inventory of raw materials		

Direct labour

Complete the following working schedule for direct labour. Each unit takes 7.5 minutes to make. There are 20 direct labour employees, each working 160 basic hours in the month. Additional hours are paid at an overtime rate of time and a half. The overtime premium is included in the direct labour cost.

Direct labour	Hours	Cost £
Basic time at £14 per hour		
Overtime		
Total		

Overheads

Complete the following working schedule for overheads. Variable overheads are recovered based on total labour hours worked.

Overheads	Hours	Cost £
Variable overheads at £9.00 per hour		
Fixed overheads		24,500
Total overheads		

(b) Complete the following operating budget, using information from the earlier tasks. Closing inventory of finished goods is to be valued at budgeted production cost per unit.

Operating budget	Units	£ per unit	£
Sales		10.50	
Cost of goods sold:			
Opening inventory of finished goods			26,475
Cost of production:		£	
Raw materials			
Direct labour			
Production overheads			
Total cost of production			
Closing inventory of finished goods			
Cost of goods sold			
Gross profit			
Non-production overheads		£	
Administration		18,000	
Marketing		13,500	
Total non-production overheads			
Net profit			

(c) Complete the cash flow forecast using the budget data that you have calculated in parts (a) and (b) of this task and the additional information below.

Enter receipts and payments as positive figures.

- The sales receivables balance is expected to increase by £8,000
- The materials payable balance is expected to decrease by £5,000
- All other payments are made in the month in which they are incurred.
- Production overheads include a depreciation charge of £7,000

Cash flow forecast	£	£
Opening cash balance		19,500
Sales receipts		
Payments:		
Materials		
Direct labour		
Production overheads		
Other overheads		
Capital expenditure	23,000	
Total payments		
Closing cash balance		

Task 4

You have prepared a draft budget for direct material costs.

- The company uses standard costing, and updates the standards annually.

- The budget is based on the current standard cost of material, but the usage of material is based on a reduction in wastage due to new machinery.

- The chief buyer has confirmed that prices are expected to remain stable.

- The production manager has confirmed the percentage saving in usage that will be incorporated into the standard for next year.

- You have calculated the total required material usage from the agreed production budget.

- You understand that there are no planned changes to raw material inventory levels.

- You have been asked to suggest appropriate performance measures that would assist managers to monitor direct material costs against budget.

Direct material budget

	This year	Next year's budget
Production units	250,000	240,000
Standard quantity of materials per unit (kg)	0.75	0.735
Total material usage (kg)	187,500	176,400
Cost of raw materials used (£)	£1,368,750	£1,287,720

Write an email to the Production Director:

(a) Explaining the calculations and assumptions and requesting his approval.

(b) Suggesting appropriate direct material performance indicators for this department.

A blank email is provided on the next page.

Email

To:

From:

Date:

Subject:

Task 5

(a) Select the appropriate term from the options given to match each of the descriptions.

Descriptions	Term	
Budgets that are continually extended into the future as time moves forward	Incremental budgets	
	Flexible budgets	
	Rolling budgets	
	Activity based budgets	
Setting selling prices at a high level to maximise profit per unit	Price skimming	
	Penetration pricing	
	Standard pricing	
	Cost plus pricing	

(b) The following information is available about a company that makes a single product.

- Each unit is made from 2.5 kg of material costing £2.80 per kg.

- It takes 10 minutes to make each item.

- 1,200 hours of basic labour time is available in the month of May. Any extra hours must be worked in overtime.

- The basic labour rate is £10 per hour. Overtime is paid at time and a half (50% more than basic rate).

- Variable overhead relates to labour hours worked, including overtime.

- Fixed overhead costs are incurred evenly through the year.

Complete the following table with the May budget figures.

	Budget for the year	Budget for May
Units sold	105,000	9,000
Units produced	100,000	8,100
	£	£
Sales	1,260,000	
Cost of production:		
Materials used	700,000	
Labour	175,000	
Variable production overhead	20,000	
Fixed production overhead	48,000	

(c) A company has already produced budgets based on its first scenario.

Assumptions in the first scenario:

- Materials and labour are variable costs
- Depreciation is a stepped fixed cost increasing every 25,000 units
- Energy costs is semi-variable, with a fixed element of £37,000
- Occupancy costs behave as fixed costs

The alternative scenario is based on:

- A decrease in selling price of 2%
- An increase in sales volume of 8%
- An increase in only the variable cost of energy of 2%
- An increase in occupancy costs of 4.5%

Apart from the selling price per unit, do not enter any decimals. Round to the nearest whole number if necessary.

Operating budget	First scenario	Alternative scenario
Selling price per unit	£15.00	£14.70
Sales volume	130,000	140,400
	£	£
Sales revenue	1,950,000	2,063,880
Costs:		
Materials	585,000	631,800
Labour	390,000	421,200
Depreciation	180,000	180,000
Energy	115,000	122,925
Occupancy costs	189,400	197,923
Total costs	1,459,400	1,553,848
Operating profit	490,600	510,032
Increase / (decrease) in profit		19,432

Complete the alternative scenario column in the operating budget table and calculate the increase or decrease in expected profit.

Task 6

(a) Select the appropriate term from the options given to match the description.

Description	Term	
The difference between the expected and actual cost of direct materials that is due to using a different quantity of materials than standard	Direct material price variance	
	Direct material usage variance	
	Direct material cost variance	
	Direct material efficiency variance	

(b) The operating statement for June showed that the direct raw material costs were £26,895. 3,300 kilos of material were used and 5,500 items were produced. The standard cost allows 0.58 kilos of material for each item, at a standard price of £8.00 per kilo.

Complete the following table, and show whether each variance is favourable or adverse.

Direct raw material costs		Fav / Adv
Flexed budget (standard cost)	£	
Actual price per kilo (to £0.01)	£	
Actual material used per item	kg	
Price variance	£	
Usage variance	£	
Cost variance	£	
Cost variance % (to 0.1%)	%	

(c) Prepare the direct labour cost statement from the activity data provided.

Round to the nearest whole number if necessary. Show adverse variances as negative amounts.

Activity data	Items produced	Labour hours	Cost £
Budget	19,500	7,800	140,400
Actual results	17,500	7,000	122,500

Direct labour cost statement	£
Standard labour cost of production	
Labour rate variance	
Labour efficiency variance	
Labour cost variance	

Task 7

The operating statement that forms part of the following table has been produced using the original fixed budget (based on production and sales of 90,000 units) and the actual costs which occurred when 80,000 units were produced and sold.

Using the data in the operating statement, together with the notes shown below, complete the flexed budget and variances in the appropriate columns in the table.

	Original budget	Actual	Flexed budget	Variances Fav / (Adv)
Volume (units)	90,000	80,000	80,000	
	£	£	£	£
Sales revenue	1,170,000	1,056,000	1,040,000	16,000
Costs:				
Materials	450,000	410,000	400,000	(10,000)
Labour	360,000	340,000	320,000	(20,000)
Distribution	180,000	155,000	160,000	5,000
Energy	55,000	55,000	50,000	(5,000)
Equipment hire	16,000	15,000	14,000	(1,000)
Depreciation	23,000	24,000	23,000	(1,000)
Marketing	21,000	20,000	21,000	1,000
Administration	25,000	24,000	25,000	1,000
Total costs	1,130,000	1,043,000	1,013,000	(30,000)
Operating profit	40,000	13,000	27,000	(14,000)

Notes on budget:

- Material, labour and distribution costs are variable.
- The budget for energy is semi-variable. The fixed element is £10,000.
- Equipment hire budget is based on a cost of £2,000 for each 12,000 units or fewer.
- Depreciation, marketing and administration costs are fixed.

Task 8

The following operating statement has been prepared using marginal costing and a flexed budget.

Operating statement for November	Budget £	Actual £	Variance £ Fav / (Adv)
Sales revenue	144,000	132,000	(12,000)
Variable costs:			
Materials	48,000	45,000	3,000
Labour	24,000	28,500	(4,500)
Distribution	12,000	12,000	0
Power	9,000	8,850	150
Contribution	**51,000**	**37,650**	**(13,350)**
Fixed costs:			
Power	3,750	4,500	(750)
Depreciation	5,250	4,950	300
Marketing	7,500	7,500	0
Administration	9,750	9,750	0
Operating profit	**24,750**	**10,950**	**(13,800)**

The original budget was based on producing and selling 1,500 units. The company actually produced and sold 1,600 units, and the budget was flexed to this volume.

You have also established the following information about the operations:

- the price of material was in line with the budgeted price

- employees worked overtime to cope with the additional output

- there was a change in both fixed and variable power costs imposed by the power supply company

- the estimated remaining lives of some non-current assets were reassessed and extended

- depreciation is calculated on a straight-line basis

Write an email to the Managing Director that suggests possible reasons for each of the variances.

Email

To:

From:

Date:

Subject:

Practice assessment 2

Task 1

(a) Match the data in the first column with the appropriate source in the second column.

Data
Amount of planned dividend payment
Details planned output levels
Demographic details of locality

Source
Market research
SWOT analysis
Suppliers' quotations
Minutes of board meeting
Production schedules
Office for National Statistics
Trade publications
HMRC website

(b) Who would you contact in each of the following situations?

(a) You want to know details of planned pay rises	
(b) You want details of planned production labour overtime	
(c) You want to know how many items are expected to be sold next month	

Select from:

1   Production Planning Manager

2   Purchasing Manager

3   Budget Committee

4   Sales Director

5   Human Resources Manager

6   Marketing Manager

7   Training Manager

(c)   For the following costs, select the most appropriate accounting treatment from the list below.

Costs:

(a)	Direct labour idle time	
(b)	Raw materials usage	
(c)	Interest on bank loan	
(d)	Repairs to roof of factory and office building	
(e)	Costs of running stores department	
(f)	Interest charge for machinery acquired on finance lease	
(g)	Direct labour productive time	
(h)	Maintenance of factory machinery	

Accounting treatments:

1   Direct production cost

2   Allocate to production overheads

3   Apportion to indirect costs of production and administration

4   Activity based charge to units of production

5   Allocate to indirect administration costs

6   Allocate to indirect finance costs

(d)   Select the most appropriate term to match these descriptions from the list that follows:

Descriptions:

(a)	A cost that remains constant in total for a limited range of output volume, and then moves to various higher amounts for higher volume levels	
(b)	A collection of main budgets including budgeted statement of profit or loss and budgeted statement of financial position	
(c)	A system where budgets are imposed on the organisation by senior managers	
(d)	A type of sampling that can be used when a sampling frame cannot be established	
(e)	A technique that can be used alongside budgeting where expected costs are calculated for each product and its components	

List of Terms:

1	Participative budgeting		7	Top down budgeting
2	Variable cost		8	Fixed cost
3	Standard costing		9	Master budget
4	Cash budget		10	Bottom up budgeting
5	Random sampling		11	Quasi-random sampling
6	Stepped fixed cost			

(e) **Stratified sampling**

Calculate the number of customers to be interviewed from each part of the country to obtain a representative response from 800 interviews. Do not show decimals. Round to the nearest whole number.

Location	North East	North West	West Midlands	East Midlands	South East	South West	Total
Number of customers	23,500	17,800	28,000	22,000	41,000	18,000	
Sample							

Task 2

(a) Complete the following production forecast for a product based on the information below. Do not show decimals. Round any decimal figures up to the next whole number of units.

Closing inventory should be 18% of the following week's sales volume. 13.5% of all production fails quality control checks and is rejected.

Production *(units)*	Week 1	Week 2	Week 3	Week 4	Week 5
Sales volume	750	800	730	745	755
Opening inventory	126				
Closing inventory					
Saleable production					
Rejected production					
Total manufactured units					

(b) Calculate raw material requirements. Do not show decimals. Round any decimal figures up to the next whole number of kilograms.

950 units of a product are to be manufactured next week.

Each unit requires 2.26 kilograms of raw material.

7.5% of raw material is wasted during manufacture.

The opening inventory will be 550 kilograms.

The closing inventory will be 700 kilograms.

	Kilograms
Raw materials required for production	
Raw materials to be purchased	

(c) Calculate labour hours. Do not show decimals. Round any decimal figures up to the next whole number of hours.

73,500 units of a product are to be made in July.

Each unit takes 3.5 minutes to produce.

21 staff will each work 180 basic hours.

	Hours
Overtime required to complete the work	

(d) Calculate sub-contracting requirements. Do not show decimals. Round any decimal figures up to the next whole number of units.

5,630 units of a product are to be manufactured next week.

Each unit takes 2.5 minutes to produce.

200 production labour hours are available.

Any additional requirement must be sub-contracted.

	Units
Work to be sub-contracted	

(e) Calculate the capacity constraints for product FX by completing the table below. Round down to the maximum whole number of units if necessary.

According to the standard cost card, each unit of FX requires 3.6 kilograms of material, 15 minutes of direct labour time and 6 minutes of machine time.

Budgets have been drafted which show the following:

Maximum sales demand of 1,000 units

Material available of 3,450 kilograms

Basic rate direct labour available (excluding overtime) of 220 hours

Machine time available of 130 hours.

Production capacity	Units
Based on material available	
Based on direct labour hours (without overtime)	
Based on available machine time	
Maximum sales volume, without using overtime	
Maximum sales volume, using unlimited overtime	

Task 3

Operating Budget

Enter the missing figures in the working schedules and operating budget using the data from the production budget and the notes below.

Production Budget	Units
Opening inventory of finished goods	43,500
Production	195,000
Sub-total	238,500
Sales	200,000
Closing inventory of finished goods	38,500

(a)   Complete these three working schedules.

Materials

Each unit produced requires 0.6 kg of material.

Closing inventory will be valued at the budgeted purchase price.

Materials	kg	£
Opening inventory	30,000	24,000
Purchases	120,000	102,000
Sub-total	150,000	126,000
Used in production		
Closing inventory		

Labour

Each item takes six minutes to produce. 120 staff each work 150 basic hours in the period. Overtime is paid at 1/3 above the basic hourly rate.

Labour	Hours	£
Basic time at £15 per hour		
Overtime		
Total		

Overheads

Variable overhead is recovered on total labour hours.

Overheads	Hours	£
Variable overheads at £5 per hour		
Fixed overheads		323,550
Total overheads		

(b)   Now complete the operating budget. Enter all amounts as positive figures. Closing finished goods inventory will be valued at the budgeted production cost per unit.

Operating Budget	Units	£ per unit	£
Sales revenue		7.00	
Cost of goods sold			£
Opening inventory of finished goods			174,000
Cost of production		£	
Materials			
Labour			
Overhead			
Closing inventory of finished goods			
Cost of goods sold			
Gross profit			
Non-production overheads		£	
Administration		253,100	
Marketing		120,500	373,600
Operating profit			

(c)   Complete the cash flow forecast using the budget data that you have calculated in parts (a) and (b) of this task and the additional information below.

Enter receipts and payments as positive figures.

- The sales receivables balance is expected to decrease by £12,000
- The materials payable balance is expected to decrease by £4,500
- All other payments are made in the period in which they are incurred.
- Production overheads include a depreciation charge of £9,000

Cash flow forecast	£	£
Opening cash balance		6,800
Sales receipts		
Payments:		
Materials		
Direct labour		
Production overheads		
Other overheads		
Capital expenditure	14,000	
Total payments		
Closing cash balance		

Task 4

Budget submission

You have prepared a draft direct labour budget for the coming year.

Background information:

·   The production budget (units) has already been agreed.

·   The Production Manager and the Training Manager have agreed to implement a new training programme.

·   The training should reduce the labour time taken to produce each unit, and this should also reduce the number of overtime hours used.

·   The basic hourly rate of pay will be increased by 2% from the start of the year.

·   You have been asked to recommend performance indicators that can be used to monitor labour performance and costs.

Draft direct labour budget	This year actual	Next year's budget
Production units	945,000	953,250
Production units per labour hour	20	20.5
Basic rate labour hours	44,000	44,000
Overtime labour hours	3,250	2,500
Basic rate labour cost	£704,000	£718,080
Overtime labour cost	£78,000	£61,200
Total labour cost	£782,000	£779,280

Write an email to the budget committee in two parts:

(a)   Requesting approval of the budget and explaining the assumptions upon which it is based.

(b)   Suggesting four appropriate performance indicators (other than cost variances) to monitor labour costs.

Email

To: The Budget Committee

From: Budget Accountant

Date: Today

Subject: Draft Direct Labour Budget

(a) Budget Submission

(b) Performance Indicators

Task 5

(a) Select the appropriate term from the options given to match each of the descriptions.

Descriptions	Term	
Using information about the current performance of an organisation to help create future budgets	Feedback	
	Control action	
	Feedforward	
	Goal congruence	
Decision making by individuals that is in their own interests, but not in the interests of the organisation	Participative budgeting	
	Goal congruence	
	Budgetary slack	
	Dysfunctional behaviour	

(b) Break a budget down into accounting periods.

Calculate the sales revenue and cost budgets for March using the budgeted unit data and the information below.

- Each unit is made from 1.6 kg of material costing £0.60 per kg.
- It takes three minutes to make each item.
- 1,500 hours of basic time are available in the month. Any extra hours must be worked in overtime.
- The basic rate is £12 per hour. Overtime is paid at £18 per hour.
- Variable overhead relates to labour hours, including overtime.
- Fixed production overhead costs are spread evenly through the year.

Budgeted units	Year	March
Units sold	360,000	28,000
Units produced	380,000	35,000
Budget in £	**Year**	**March**
Sales revenue	1,260,000	
Material used	364,800	
Direct labour	250,000	
Variable production overhead	95,000	
Fixed production overhead	252,000	

(c)   Budget revision

You have submitted a draft operating budget to the budget committee. The committee have asked you to prepare a budget for an alternative scenario and calculate the increase or decrease in expected profit.

Complete the alternative scenario column in the operating budget table and calculate the increase or decrease in profit.

Assumptions in the first scenario:

- Material and labour are the only variable costs
- There is an allowance for an energy price rise of 7%
- Other production overheads are a stepped fixed cost, increasing at every 10,000 units

Alternative scenario:

- The selling price is reduced by 5%
- The sales volume rises by 12%
- The energy price rise is to be budgeted at 9%

Apart from the selling price per unit, do not enter decimals. Round to the nearest whole number if necessary.

Operating budget	First draft	Alternative scenario
Sales price per unit	£12.00	
Sales volume	144,000	
	£	£
Sales revenue	1,728,000	
Costs:		
Material	648,000	
Labour	360,000	
Energy	16,050	
Other production overheads	450,000	
Total costs	1,474,050	
Gross profit	253,950	
Increase / (decrease) in gross profit		

Task 6

(a)   Select the appropriate term from the options given to match the description.

Descriptions	Term	
The manager responsible for a specific budget and the actual performance that is measured against that budget	Budget accountant	
	Budget holder	
	Budget committee	
	Budget manual	

(b)   **Variance analysis**

Prepare the direct material cost statement from the activity data provided.

Enter any adverse variances using a minus (–) sign.

Activity data	Items produced	Kilograms material	Cost
			£
Budget	12,000	30,000	37,500
Actual	14,000	38,500	40,000

Direct material cost statement	£
Standard direct material cost of production	
Variances:	
Material price	
Material usage	
Material cost	

(c)   Prepare the direct labour cost statement from the activity data provided.

Round to the nearest whole number if necessary. Show adverse variances as negative amounts.

Activity data	Items produced	Labour hours	Cost £
Budget	12,500	17,500	332,500
Actual results	13,100	19,250	341,900

Direct labour cost statement	£
Standard labour cost of production	348,460
Labour rate variance	23,850
Labour efficiency variance	−17,290
Labour cost variance	6,560

Task 7

Operating report

You are required to complete the monthly operating report below. Flex the budget, calculate variances and show whether each variance is favourable or adverse by denoting adverse variances with minus signs. The original budget and actual results have been entered.

Notes:

Materials, labour and distribution costs are variable.

Energy cost is semi-variable. The variable element is £0.50 per unit.

Equipment hire is a stepped cost, budgeted to increase uniformly at every 20,000 units of production.

Depreciation, marketing and administration costs are fixed.

Original budget		Flexed budget	Actual	Variance
121,000	**Sales volume (units)**		105,000	
£		£	£	£
1,452,000	Sales revenue		1,270,500	
	Costs:			
242,000	Materials		207,900	
302,500	Labour		264,600	
181,500	Distribution		158,550	
80,000	Energy		78,000	
91,000	Equipment hire		86,350	
81,300	Depreciation		82,000	
105,000	Marketing		115,250	
63,400	Administration		62,800	
1,146,700	Total costs		1,055,450	
305,300	Operating profit (loss)		215,050	

Task 8

Operational review

Review the operating statement shown below together with the additional information, and prepare an email report.

Additional information:

The budget has been flexed to the actual number of units produced and sold. The original budget was based on an expected sales volume of 220,000 units which was expected to generate a profit of £363,000.

A major competitor unexpectedly ceased trading at the beginning of the period. The company was able to take advantage of the situation through a marketing promotion and increased production and sales by 20%.

Some employees who previously worked for the competitor were taken on to help cope with the increased volume, although the differing working practices have caused some issues. Overtime working that was not budgeted for was also required.

Negotiation with the material manufacturer that previously supplied both companies has resulted in a small unit reduction in the cost price of material.

Operating statement	Flexed budget	Actual	Variances Fav / (Adv)
Sales volume		264,000	
	£000	£000	£000
Sales revenue	5,280	5,227	(53)
Variable costs:			
Material	1,584	1,601	(17)
Labour	1,980	2,055	(75)
Distribution	396	396	0
Power	528	528	0
Total variable costs	4,488	4,580	(92)
Contribution	792	647	(145)
Fixed costs:			
Depreciation	85	85	0
Marketing	110	163	(53)
Administration	102	110	(8)
Total fixed costs	297	358	(61)
Operating profit	**495**	**289**	**(206)**

Prepare a report for the budget committee that:

(a)   explains the likely causes for the variances, and

(b)   briefly notes the future opportunities and threats created by the change in market conditions.

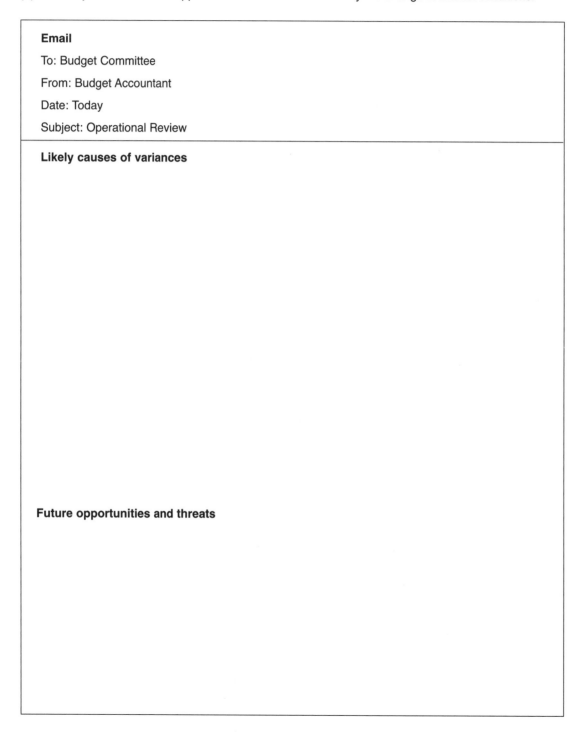

Email

To: Budget Committee

From: Budget Accountant

Date: Today

Subject: Operational Review

Likely causes of variances

Future opportunities and threats

Practice assessment 3

Task 1

(a) Match the data in the first column with the appropriate source in the second column.

Data
Customers who pay promptly
Current raw materials costs
Employers' National Insurance rates

Source
Product life cycle report
Office for National Statistics
HMRC website
Sales ledger
Supplier price lists
Trade association

(b) Who would you contact in each of the following situations?

(a) You want to know details of expected future material costs	
(b) You want to know when the factory extension will be operational	
(c) You want to know the cost of next year's advertising campaign	

Select from:

1 Factory Capital Project Manager

2 HR Manager

3 Transport Manager

4 Purchasing Manager

5 Finance Director

6 Marketing Manager

(c) Complete the following table by using ticks to show into which budget(s) each item of cost would occur.

	Capital expenditure	Cost of production	Sales and marketing	Distribution	Finance
Loan set up fees					
Celebrity product endorsement fees					
Product design royalties					
Purchase of new distribution vehicle					
Agency fees for temporary production labour					
Distribution vehicle fuel					

(d) Select an appropriate accounting treatment for each of the following costs from the options available.

Descriptions:

(a)	Employers' pension contributions for sales staff	
(b)	Product design royalties	
(c)	Repairs to factory roof	
(d)	Cost of maintaining production equipment	
(e)	Cost of sick pay for production operatives	
(f)	Cost of advertising campaign	

Options are:

1   Allocate to production overheads
2   Allocate to selling and distribution overheads
3   Direct cost
4   Allocate to finance overheads
5   Allocate to marketing overheads
6   Capital expenditure

(e)   This year's sales are £3,800,000. Analysis of recent years shows:

- a negative growth trend of −1.0% per annum

- seasonal variations from the trend of:

  Quarter 1   −£4,000

  Quarter 2   +£2,000

  Quarter 3   +£5,000

  Quarter 4   −£3,000

Forecast the sales for each quarter of next year, using the following table.

	£
Quarter 1	
Quarter 2	
Quarter 3	
Quarter 4	
Total Sales	

Task 2

(a)   Complete the following table to show the forecast inventories and production units for a particular product.

Closing inventory should be 40% of the following week's forecast sales volume.

Number of units	Week 1	Week 2	Week 3	Week 4	Week 5
Opening inventory	16,000				
Production					
Sub-total					
Forecast sales	40,000	38,500	42,000	39,500	40,000
Closing inventory					

(b) The production requirements of a product are shown below. 12% of the units produced fail a quality control test and are scrapped. Complete the table to show the number of units that must be manufactured to allow for this rejection rate.

	Month 1	Month 2	Month 3
Required units	93,720	96,272	96,800
Manufactured units			

(c) The following information is available about the plans for next month.

- 211,500 units of finished product are to be manufactured
- Each unit of finished product contains 2.3 kg of raw material
- 6% of raw material is wasted during manufacture
- The opening inventory of raw material is 48,000 kg
- The closing inventory of raw material is to be 46,500 kg

The purchases of raw material must be:

(a) 96,326 kg	
(b) 484,950 kg	
(c) 514,137 kg	
(d) 516,000 kg	
(e) 519,000 kg	

(d) 90,000 units of finished product are to be manufactured during October. Each unit takes 2.5 minutes to produce. 19 staff each work 190 basic hours in October.

Complete the following sentences:

The number of units that can be made in basic time during October is ⬚ .

The number of overtime hours required to be worked in October is ⬚ hours.

(e) Department W manufactures three products, Exe, Wye and Zed.

Calculate the machine hours required to manufacture these in November, using the following table.

Product	Units	Hours per unit	Hours required
Exe	450	2.0	
Wye	570	1.2	
Zed	400	1.0	
Total machine hours for department W			

There are seven machines in the department.

Each machine can be used for 290 hours in November. Additional machines can be hired if required.

How many additional machines should be hired?

(f) Calculate the capacity constraints for product GT by completing the table below. Round down to the maximum whole number of units if necessary.

According to the standard cost card, each unit of GT requires 4.1 kilograms of material, 66 minutes of direct labour time and 15 minutes of machine time.

Budgets have been drafted which show the following:

Maximum sales demand of 1,500 units

Material available of 6,050 kilograms

Basic rate direct labour available (excluding overtime) of 1,480 hours

Machine time available of 350 hours.

Production capacity	Units
Based on material available	
Based on direct labour hours (without overtime)	
Based on available machine time	
Maximum sales volume, without using overtime	
Maximum sales volume, using unlimited overtime	

Task 3

The following production budget for a month has been prepared.

Production budget	Units
Opening inventory of finished goods	5,000
Production	54,000
Sub-total	59,000
Sales	50,000
Closing inventory of finished goods	9,000

(a) Complete these three working schedules.

Materials

Each unit produced requires 0.75 kg of material. Closing inventory is valued at budgeted purchase price.

Raw materials	kg	£
Opening inventory of raw materials	2,300	15,450
Purchases of raw materials	40,000	210,000
Sub-total	42,300	225,450
Used in production		
Closing inventory of raw materials		

Direct Labour

Each unit takes 12 minutes to make. There are 55 direct labour employees, each working 170 basic hours in the month. Additional hours are paid at an overtime rate of time and a half. The overtime premium is included in the direct labour cost.

Direct labour	Hours	Cost £
Basic time at £18 per hour		
Overtime		
Total		

Overheads

Variable overheads are recovered based on total labour hours worked.

Overheads	Hours	Cost £
Variable overheads at £7.00 per hour		
Fixed overheads		40,950
Total overheads		

(b) Now complete the operating budget. Enter all amounts as positive figures. Closing finished goods inventory will be valued at the budgeted production cost per unit.

Operating Budget	Units	£ per unit	£
Sales		13.00	
Cost of goods sold:			£
Opening inventory of finished goods			47,500
Cost of production:		£	
Raw materials			
Direct labour			
Production overheads			
Closing inventory of finished goods			
Cost of goods sold			
Gross profit			
Non-production overheads		£	
Administration		93,500	
Marketing		48,900	
Total non-production overheads			
Operating profit/(loss)			

(c)   Complete the cash flow forecast using the budget data that you have calculated in parts (a) and (b) of this task and the additional information below.

Enter receipts and payments as positive figures.

- The sales receivables balance is expected to decrease by £42,000
- The materials payable balance is expected to increase by £34,800
- All other payments are made in the month in which they are incurred.
- Production overheads include a depreciation charge of £17,000
- Other overheads include an increase in non-cash provisions of £5,000

Cash flow forecast	£	£
Opening cash balance		110,600
Sales receipts		
Payments:		
Materials		
Direct labour		
Production overheads		
Other overheads		
Capital expenditure	73,500	
Total payments		
Closing cash balance		

Task 4

You have prepared a draft budget for direct labour costs.

- The budget is based on the expected rise in the relevant regional labour cost index of 2.2%, although the company wage negotiations for next year have not yet concluded. This information has been provided by the HR Manager.

- The Production Manager has confirmed that an efficiency saving of 1% of the labour time required to make each unit is expected due to replacement of some production machinery that is scheduled for the end of the current year.

- In the current year the direct labour hours have been fulfilled by full time employees, who did not work any overtime.

- You have calculated the total labour hours required from the agreed production budget.

- You have been asked to suggest possible inherent risks in the draft budget and its assumptions.

Direct labour budget	This year actual	Next year's budget
Production units	450,000	440,000
Labour time required to produce 1,000 units	50	49.5
Total labour hours required	22,500	21,780
Hourly rate	£12.50	£12.775
Total labour cost	£281,250	£278,240

Write an email to the Production Director:

(a)   Explaining the calculations and assumptions and requesting her approval.

(b)   Suggesting possible inherent risks in the draft budget and its assumptions.

Email

To:

From:

Date:

Subject:

Task 5

(a) Select the appropriate term from the options given to match each of the descriptions.

Descriptions	Term	
The result of budget data based on over-estimation of costs or under-estimation of income	Goal congruence	
	Budgetary slack	
	Performance related pay	
	Feedforward	
The imposition of budgets by senior managers without the participation of operational budget holders	Participative budgeting	
	Bottom-up budgeting	
	Top-down budgeting	
	Activity based budgeting	

(b) Calculate the sales revenue and cost budgets for June from the following data
- Each unit is made from 1.5 kg of material costing £1.80 per kg.
- It takes six minutes to make each item.
- 1,200 hours of basic labour time is available in the month of June. Any extra hours must be worked in overtime.
- The basic labour rate is £14 per hour. Overtime is paid at time and a half (50% more than basic rate).
- Variable overhead relates to labour hours worked, including overtime.
- Fixed overhead costs are incurred evenly through the year.

Complete the following table with the June budget figures.

	Budget for the year	Budget for June
Units sold	144,000	12,500
Units produced	150,000	13,000
	£	£
Sales	792,000	
Cost of production:		
Materials used	405,000	
Labour	220,000	
Variable production overhead	15,000	
Fixed production overhead	24,000	

(c)   You are asked to prepare a revised operating budget in the Revision column below, and calculate the increase or decrease in profit that would result.

You should assume that the selling price will be reduced by 10% and the sales volume will increase by 20%.

Draft operating budget	First draft	Revision
Sales units	120,000	
	£	£
Sales price	15.00	
Sales revenue	1,800,000	
Variable production costs	1,320,000	
Fixed production costs	130,000	
Gross profit	350,000	
Increase / (Decrease) in gross profit		

Task 6

(a)   Select the appropriate term from the options given to match the description.

Description	Term	
The standard cost variance that records the difference between the flexed direct labour budget and the actual cost of direct labour	Total direct cost variance	
	Direct labour rate variance	
	Direct labour cost variance	
	Direct material efficiency variance	

(b)   The operating statement for September showed that the direct raw material costs were £57,850. 15,974 kilos of material were used and 9,800 items were produced. The standard cost allows 1.6 kilos of material for each item, at a standard price of £3.60 per kilo.

Complete the following table, and show whether each variance is favourable or adverse.

Direct raw material costs		Fav / Adv
Flexed budget (standard cost)	£	
Actual price per kilo (to £0.01)	£	
Actual material used per item	kg	
Price variance (to nearest £)	£	
Usage variance (to nearest £)	£	
Cost variance	£	
Cost variance % (to 0.01%)	%	

(c)   Prepare the direct labour cost statement from the activity data provided.

Round to the nearest whole number if necessary. Show adverse variances as negative amounts.

Activity data	Items produced	Labour hours	Cost
			£
Budget	24,300	8,100	170,100
Actual results	23,700	8,000	165,900

Direct labour cost statement	£
Standard labour cost of production	
Labour rate variance	
Labour efficiency variance	
Labour cost variance	

Task 7

Reporting results

You are required to complete a monthly operating report for June. The original budget for the month is shown below, followed by relevant notes.

Operating budget for June	£
Sales revenue (50,000 units)	1,450,000
Costs:	
Material	550,000
Labour	325,000
Distribution	190,000
Energy	90,000
Equipment hire	40,000
Depreciation	25,000
Marketing	70,000
Administration	45,000
Total costs	1,335,000
Operating profit	115,000

Notes on budget:

- Material, labour and distribution costs are variable

- The budget for energy is semi-variable. The fixed element is £30,000

- Equipment hire budget is based on a cost of £5,000 for each 7,000 units or fewer

- Depreciation, marketing and administration costs are fixed

Complete the operating report for June shown below with actual figures already inserted. Flex the budget to the actual sales volume and calculate the variances. Show adverse variances with minus signs.

	Flexed budget £	Actual £	Variances £
Sales revenue (60,000 units)		1,710,000	
Costs:			
Materials		650,000	
Labour		404,000	
Distribution		248,000	
Energy		117,000	
Equipment hire		55,000	
Depreciation		26,000	
Marketing		69,000	
Administration		44,000	
Total Costs		1,613,000	
Operating profit		97,000	

Task 8

The following operating statement has been prepared using marginal costing and a flexed budget.

Operating statement for November	Budget	Actual	Variances Fav / (Adv)
Sales revenue	90,000	94,000	4,000
Variable costs:			
Materials	12,000	15,000	–3,000
Labour	18,000	19,000	–1,000
Distribution	20,000	22,500	–2,500
Power	10,000	13,000	–3,000
Contribution	30,000	24,500	–5,500
Fixed costs:			
Power	5,000	0	5,000
Depreciation	5,500	6,100	–600
Marketing	7,000	3,000	4,000
Administration	4,000	4,000	0
Operating profit	**8,500**	**11,400**	**2,900**

The original budget was based on producing and selling 2,500 units. The company actually produced and sold 2,000 units, and the budget was flexed to this volume.

You have also established the following information about the operations:

- the volume of material used was in line with the flexed volume
- there was some idle time by employees due to the reduced output, but the wage rate was in line with the budget
- there was an unplanned rise in vehicle fuel prices
- the company changed power supplier
- the estimated remaining lives of some non current assets was reassessed and reduced
- depreciation is calculated on a straight line basis
- a budgeted advertising campaign was scaled down

Write an email to the Managing Director that suggests possible reasons for each of the variances.

Email

To:

From:

Date:

Subject:

Answers to practice assessment 1

Task 1

(a)

Data		Source
Typical performance in the trade	➡	Trade association publications
National economic growth	➡	Office for National Statistics
Corporation tax rates	➡	HMRC publications

(b) (a) 5

(b) 4

(c) 1

(c)

	Direct cost of production	Production overheads	Capital expenditure	Marketing	Cash
Extension to offices			✔		✔
Depreciation of production equipment		✔			
Indirect production labour		✔			✔
Advertising campaign costs				✔	✔
Hire of production equipment		✔			✔
Printing customer perceptions questionnaire				✔	✔

(d) (a) 2

(b) 3

(c) 2

(d) 1

(e) 6

(f) 3

(e)

	£
Quarter 1	600,625
Quarter 2	660,625
Quarter 3	695,625
Quarter 4	605,625
Total Sales	2,562,500

Task 2

(a)

Number of Units	Week 1	Week 2	Week 3	Week 4	Week 5
Opening inventory	5,000	5,375	5,250	5,125	5,500
Production	20,375	21,375	20,875	20,875	22,750
Sub total	25,375	26,750	26,125	26,000	28,250
Forecast sales	20,000	21,500	21,000	20,500	22,000
Closing inventory	5,375	5,250	5,125	5,500	6,250

(b)

	Month 1	Month 2	Month 3
Required units	75,330	79,980	77,190
Manufactured units	81,000	86,000	83,000

(c)   (e)   102,000 kg

(d)   The number of units that can be made in basic time during October is **43,200**.

The number of overtime hours required to be worked in October is **340**.

(e)   There is labour available to make **52,500** units in normal time. Therefore, **2,500** hours of overtime will be needed.

The raw material contract will provide enough material to make **40,000** units. Therefore, **50,000** kg will have to be purchased on the open market.

Quality control can test **50,400** units in the year. It will be necessary to make alternative arrangements for **9,600** units.

Task 3

(a)

Raw materials	kg	£
Opening inventory of raw materials	1,800	7,200
Purchases of raw materials	34,000	136,000
Sub-total	35,800	143,200
Used in production	35,000	140,000
Closing inventory of raw materials	800	3,200

Direct labour	Hours	Cost £
Basic time at £14 per hour	3,200	44,800
Overtime	300	6,300
Total	3,500	51,100

Overheads	Hours	Cost £
Variable overheads at £9.00 per hour	3,500	31,500
Fixed overheads		24,500
Total overheads		56,000

(b)

Operating budget	Units	£ per unit	£
Sales	30,000	10.50	315,000
Cost of goods sold:			
Opening inventory of finished goods			26,475
Cost of production:		£	
Raw materials		140,000	
Direct labour		51,100	
Production overheads		56,000	
Total cost of production			247,100
Closing inventory of finished goods			8,825
Cost of goods sold			264,750
Gross profit			50,250
Non-production overheads		£	
Administration		18,000	
Marketing		13,500	
Total non-production overheads			31,500
Net profit			18,750

(c)

Cash flow forecast	£	£
Opening cash balance		19,500
Sales receipts		307,000
Payments:		
Materials	141,000	
Direct labour	51,100	
Production overheads	49,000	
Other overheads	31,500	
Capital expenditure	23,000	
Total payments		295,600
Closing cash balance		30,900

Task 4 (a) and **(b)**

Email	
To:	Production Director
From:	Accounting Technician
Date:	xx
Subject:	Direct Material Budget

Budget Submission

I enclose the proposed direct material budget for your consideration and approval.

The production budget is based on a decrease from the current output of 250,000 units to 240,000 units next year, and this assumption has been used for the direct material budget.

The budget assumes the current standard usage of raw material per unit produced of 0.75 kg will be reduced by 2% to 0.735 kg. This change will be incorporated into the revised standards for next year. The chief buyer has confirmed that the cost price of material is not expected to change next year, and therefore the standard cost per kg will remain the same as the current cost of £7.30 per kg.

Since there is no planned change in the raw material inventory levels, the quantity of material to be purchased will be the same as the budgeted usage.

Please let me know if you need any further information.

Performance Indicators

As the company uses standard costing, the material cost variances will be a very useful performance indicator. The variances are:

- direct material price variance
- direct material usage variance

These variances could be prepared weekly or monthly. The direct material price variance will show the difference in the material cost for the period compared to the standard that is due to the price of material. The direct material usage variance will show the difference that is due to the amount of material used. Since there is an expectation that wastage will be reduced in the next year, the usage variance will be particularly helpful in monitoring this aspect.

Task 5

(a)

Descriptions	Term	
Budgets that are continually extended into the future as time moves forward	Incremental budgets	
	Flexible budgets	
	Rolling budgets	✔
	Activity based budgets	
Setting selling prices at a high level to maximise profit per unit	Price skimming	✔
	Penetration pricing	
	Standard pricing	
	Cost plus pricing	

(b)

	Budget for the year	Budget for May
Units sold	105,000	9,000
Units produced	100,000	8,100
	£	£
Sales	1,260,000	108,000
Cost of production:		
Materials used	700,000	56,700
Labour	175,000	14,250
Variable production overhead	20,000	1,620
Fixed production overhead	48,000	4,000

(c)

Operating budget	First scenario	Alternative scenario
Selling price per unit	£15.00	£14.70
Sales volume	130,000	140,400
	£	£
Sales revenue	1,950,000	2,063,880
Costs:		
Materials	585,000	631,800
Labour	390,000	421,200
Depreciation	180,000	180,000
Energy	115,000	122,925
Occupancy costs	189,400	197,923
Total costs	1,459,400	1,553,848
Operating profit	490,600	510,032
Increase / (decrease) in profit		19,432

Task 6

(a)

Description	Term	
The difference between the expected and actual cost of direct materials that is due to using a different quantity of materials than standard	Direct material price variance	
	Direct material usage variance	✔
	Direct material cost variance	
	Direct material efficiency variance	

(b)

Direct raw material costs		Fav / Adv
Flexed budget (standard cost)	£25,520	
Actual price per kilo (to £0.01)	£8.15	
Actual material used per item	0.6 kg	
Price variance	£495	Adv
Usage variance	£880	Adv
Cost variance	£1,375	Adv
Cost variance % (to 0.1%)	5.4%	

(c)

Direct labour cost statement	£
Standard labour cost of production	126,000
Labour rate variance	3,500
Labour efficiency variance	0
Labour cost variance	3,500

Task 7

	Original budget	Actual	Flexed budget	Variances Fav / (Adv)
Volume (units)	90,000	80,000	80,000	
	£	£	£	£
Sales revnue	1,170,000	1,056,000	1,040,000	16,000
Costs:				
Materials	450,000	410,000	400,000	(10,000)
Labour	360,000	340,000	320,000	(20,000)
Distribution	180,000	155,000	160,000	5,000
Energy	55,000	55,000	50,000	(5,000)
Equipment hire	16,000	15,000	14,000	(1,000)
Depreciation	23,000	24,000	23,000	(1,000)
Marketing	21,000	20,000	21,000	1,000
Administration	25,000	24,000	25,000	1,000
Total costs	1,130,000	1,043,000	1,013,000	(30,000)
Operating profit	40,000	13,000	27,000	(14,000)

Task 8

Email

To: Managing Director

From: Accounting Technician

Subject: Operating Statement For November

Date: xx

I attach the operating statement for November. This has been prepared using a budget flexed to the actual production and sales volume of 1,600 units. This is an increase on the original budget which was based on 1,500 units.

As can be seen from the statement, the actual operating profit was considerably lower than that shown on the flexed budget. The following commentary will suggest possible reasons for each of the variances that analyse this difference.

The adverse sales revenue variance was caused by selling at a lower average price than budgeted (£82.50 instead of £90). This may have helped increase the sales from the original budget.

It has been established that the price paid for materials was in line with the budgeted price. The favourable material variance must therefore be due to using less material than expected for the output achieved. This could be due to less wastage than was allowed for.

A possible cause of the adverse labour cost variance is the need to use overtime hours, which are traditionally paid at a higher hourly rate than basic hours. The additional hours would be required due to the additional production volume that was achieved.

The changes in the power tariff mean that a greater element of the cost is fixed than budgeted, although the variable element has decreased. Overall the total power cost has increased. Although possible changes in power consumption should be investigated, it seems likely that the variances are caused by the alteration to the tariff.

The actual depreciation charge is lower than that budgeted since the expected remaining lives of some non-current assets have been reassessed to a longer period, and the depreciation charge using the straight-line basis is therefore reduced. This change can be incorporated into future budgets.

In summary, the overall operating profit adverse variance is mainly accounted for by the reduction in average selling price compared to budget.

Answers to practice assessment 2

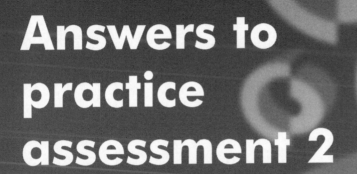

Task 1

(a)

Data		Source
Amount of planned dividend payment	➤	Minutes of board meeting
Details planned output levels	➤	Production schedules
Demographic details of locality	➤	Office for National Statistics

(b) (a) 5
     (b) 1
     (c) 4

(c) (a) 2
     (b) 1
     (c) 6
     (d) 3
     (e) 4
     (f) 6
     (g) 1
     (h) 2

(d) (a) 6
     (b) 9
     (c) 7
     (d) 11
     (e) 3

(e)

Location	North East	North West	West Midlands	East Midlands	South East	South West	Total
Number of customers	23,500	17,800	28,000	22,000	41,000	18,000	150,300
Sample	125	95	149	117	218	96	800

Task 2

(a)

Number of Units	Week 1	Week 2	Week 3	Week 4	Week 5
Sales volume	750	800	730	745	755
Opening inventory	126	144	132	135	
Closing inventory	144	132	135	136	
Saleable production	768	788	733	746	
Rejected production	120	123	115	117	
Total manufactured units	888	911	848	863	

(b)

	Kilograms
Raw materials required for production	2,322
Raw materials to be purchased	2,472

(c)

	Hours
Overtime required to complete the work	508

(d)

	Units
Work to be sub-contracted	830

(e)

Production capacity	Units
Based on material available	958
Based on direct labour hours (without overtime)	880
Based on available machine time	1,300
Maximum sales volume, without using overtime	880
Maximum sales volume, using unlimited overtime	958

Task 3

(a)

Materials

Materials	kg	£
Opening inventory	30,000	24,000
Purchases	120,000	102,000
Sub-total	150,000	126,000
Used in production	117,000	97,950
Closing inventory	33,000	28,050

Labour

Labour	Hours	£
Basic time at £15 per hour	18,000	270,000
Overtime	1,500	30,000
Total	19,500	300,000

Overheads

Overhead	Hours	£
Variable overheads at £5 per hour	19,500	97,500
Fixed overheads		323,550
Total overheads		421,050

(b)

Operating Budget	Units	£ per unit	£
Sales revenue	200,000	7.00	1,400,000
Cost of goods sold			£
Opening inventory of finished goods			174,000
Cost of production		£	
Materials		97,950	
Labour		300,000	
Overhead		421,050	819,000
Closing inventory of finished goods			161,700
Cost of goods sold			831,300
Gross profit			568,700
Non-production overheads		£	
Administration		253,100	
Marketing		120,500	373,600
Operating profit			195,100

(c)

Cash flow forecast	£	£
Opening cash balance		6,800
Sales receipts		1,412,000
Payments:		
Materials	106,500	
Direct labour	300,000	
Production overheads	412,050	
Other overheads	373,600	
Capital expenditure	14,000	
Total payments		1,206,150
Closing cash balance		212,650

Task 4

Email
To: The Budget Committee
From: Budget Accountant
Date: Today
Subject: Draft Direct Labour Budget

(a)   Budget Submission

I attach the proposed direct labour budget for next year for your consideration and approval. This year's results are shown for comparison.

The draft budget is based on the agreed production budget of 953,250 units which is slightly less than a 1% increase over the current year.

The planned training programme that has been agreed by the Production Manager and the Training Manager will be implemented, and this should result in an increased output per labour hour of 2.5%. Because of this, the total number of labour hours required is planned to reduce from 47,250 to 46,500 despite the slightly increased total production output.

The number of labour hours to be used at basic rate is unchanged, and there is a reduction in the requirement of overtime hours.

The planned pay increase of 2% has been incorporated into the budget. This brings the basic labour rate to £16.32 per hour, and the overtime rate to £24.48 per hour.

Overall the budgeted total labour cost for next year is slightly less than the current year. The budgeted direct labour cost per unit is approximately £0.8175 compared with the current year figure of £0.8275.

(b)   Performance Indicators

The validity of the budget depends heavily on the increased productivity of the labour force following the training programme. The following performance indicators are recommended for use:

*   average units produced per direct labour hour
*   number of overtime hours worked
*   overtime hours as a percentage of total labour hours
*   total direct labour cost per unit produced

Task 5

(a)

Descriptions	Term	
Using information about the current performance of an organisation to help create future budgets	Feedback	
	Control action	
	Feedforward	✔
	Goal congruence	
Decision making by individuals that is in their own interests, but not in the interests of the organisation	Participative budgeting	
	Goal congruence	
	Budgetary slack	
	Dysfunctional behaviour	✔

(b)

Budgeted units	Year	March
Units sold	360,000	28,000
Units produced	380,000	35,000
Budget in £	**Year**	**March**
Sales revenue	1,260,000	98,000
Material used	364,800	33,600
Direct labour	250,000	22,500
Variable production overhead	95,000	8,750
Fixed production overhead	252,000	21,000

(c)

Operating budget	First draft	Alternative scenario
Sales price per unit	£12.00	£11.40
Sales volume	144,000	161,280
	£	£
Sales revenue	1,728,000	1,838,592
Costs:		
Material	648,000	725,760
Labour	360,000	403,200
Energy	16,050	16,350
Other production overheads	450,000	510,000
Total costs	1,474,050	1,655,310
Gross profit	253,950	183,282
Increase / (decrease) in gross profit		(70,668)

Task 6

(a)

Description	Term	
The manager responsible for a specific budget and the actual performance that is measured against that budget	Budget accountant	
	Budget holder	✔
	Budget committee	
	Budget manual	

(b)

Direct material cost statement	£
Standard direct material cost of production	43,750
Variances:	
Material price	8,125
Material usage	−4,375
Material cost	3,750

(c)

Direct labour cost statement	£
Standard labour cost of production	348,460
Labour rate variance	23,850
Labour efficiency variance	−17,290
Labour cost variance	6,560

Task 7

Original budget		Flexed budget	Actual	Variance
121,000	**Sales volume (units)**		105,000	
£		£	£	£
1,452,000	Sales revenue	1,260,000	1,270,500	10,500
	Costs:			
242,000	Materials	210,000	207,900	2,100
302,500	Labour	262,500	264,600	−2,100
181,500	Distribution	157,500	158,550	−1,050
80,000	Energy	72,000	78,000	−6,000
91,000	Equipment hire	78,000	86,350	−8,350
81,300	Depreciation	81,300	82,000	−700
105,000	Marketing	105,000	115,250	−10,250
63,400	Administration	63,400	62,800	600
1,146,700	Total costs	1,029,700	1,055,450	−25,750
305,300	Operating profit (loss)	230,300	215,050	−15,250

Task 8(a) and **(b)**

Email

To: Budget Committee

From: Budget Accountant

Date: Today

Subject: Operational Review

Likely causes of variances

I have reviewed the results for the period. There was an operating profit of £289,000 compared with the flexed budget profit of £495,000. The original budgeted profit was £363,000 which was calculated without the increase in sales volume of 20% which has occurred.

There are adverse variances in sales revenue, material and labour variable costs, and marketing and administration costs. There are no favourable variances.

The sales revenue variance of £53,000 must have been caused by a reduction in selling price compared with the budget. This equates to an average price reduction of about 20 pence (1%) on each unit that we planned to sell for £20.

The material variance of £17,000 was disappointing, especially after a small price reduction had been negotiated with the supplier. This variance must be the result of an adverse usage variance that was greater than the benefit of the price reduction. There may be a link with the integration of new employees who were used to different working practices.

The labour variance of £75,000 could be caused by a combination of two factors. Firstly, the integration of new employees mentioned above may have resulted in inefficient working. Secondly, there was a requirement for unbudgeted overtime working which would have been at a premium rate. Both these issues are as a result of the increase in production above the original plan.

The marketing variance of £53,000 was probably caused by the promotion to sell to previous customers of the competitor that has ceased trading. The administration variance of £8,000 is likely to be a consequence of the increased volume creating a step in what would otherwise be a fixed cost.

Future opportunities and threats

It is clear from the outcome of the year's performance that the elimination of a competitor from the marketplace has not been entirely beneficial. While there may be opportunities to further increase volume, if a close control is not kept on costs then the results will not be worthwhile.

The reason for the competitor's closure should be carefully examined. If it is the result of a contraction in the whole market, or other issues that could impact on this organisation then these must be considered for the future.

Answers to practice assessment 3

Task 1

(a)

Data		Source
Customers who pay promptly	➤	Sales ledger
Current raw materials costs	➤	Supplier price lists
Employers' National Insurance rates	➤	HMRC website

(b)

(a) 4

(b) 1

(c) 6

(c)

	Capital expenditure	Cost of production	Sales and marketing	Distribution	Finance
Loan set up fees					✔
Celebrity product endorsement fees			✔		
Product design royalties		✔			
Purchase of new distribution vehicle	✔				
Agency fees for temporary production labour		✔			
Distribution vehicle fuel				✔	

(d)

(a) 2

(b) 3

(c) 1

(d) 1

(e) 1

(f) 5

(e)

	£
Quarter 1	936,500
Quarter 2	942,500
Quarter 3	945,500
Quarter 4	937,500
Total Sales	3,762,000

Task 2

(a)

Number of Units	Week 1	Week 2	Week 3	Week 4	Week 5
Opening inventory	16,000	15,400	16,800	15,800	
Production	39,400	39,900	41,000	39,700	
Sub-total	55,400	55,300	57,800	55,500	
Forecast sales	40,000	38,500	42,000	39,500	40,000
Closing inventory	15,400	16,800	15,800	16,000	

(b)

	Month 1	Month 2	Month 3
Required units	93,720	96,272	96,800
Manufactured units	106,500	109,400	110,000

(c)   **(d)**   516,000 kg

(d)   The number of units that can be made in basic time during October is **86,640**.

The number of overtime hours required to be worked in October is **140** hours.

(e)

Product	Units	Hours per unit	Hours required
Exe	450	2.0	900
Wye	570	1.2	684
Zed	400	1.0	400
Total machine hours for department W			1,984

No additional machines should be hired.

(f)

Production capacity	Units
Based on material available	1,475
Based on direct labour hours (without overtime)	1,345
Based on available machine time	1,400
Maximum sales volume, without using overtime	1,345
Maximum sales volume, using unlimited overtime	1,400

Task 3

(a)   Materials

Raw Materials	kg	£
Opening inventory of raw materials	2,300	15,450
Purchases of raw materials	40,000	210,000
Sub-total	42,300	225,450
Used in production	40,500	216,000
Closing inventory of raw materials	1,800	9,450

Direct Labour

Direct Labour	Hours	Cost £
Basic time at £18 per hour	9,350	168,300
Overtime	1,450	39,150
Total	10,800	207,450

Overheads

Overheads	Hours	Cost £
Variable overheads at £7.00 per hour	10,800	75,600
Fixed overheads		40,950
Total overheads		116,550

(b)

Operating Budget	Units	£ per unit	£
Sales	50,000	13.00	650,000
Cost of Goods Sold:			
Opening inventory of finished goods			47,500
Cost of production:		£	
Raw Materials		216,000	
Direct Labour		207,450	
Production Overheads		116,550	
Total cost of production			540,000
Closing inventory of finished goods			90,000
Cost of goods sold			497,500
Gross profit			152,500
Non-production overheads		£	
Administration		93,500	
Marketing		48,900	
Total non-production overheads			142,400
Operating profit / (loss)			10,100

(c)

Cash flow forecast	£	£
Opening cash balance		110,600
Sales receipts		692,000
Payments:		
Materials	175,200	
Direct labour	207,450	
Production overheads	99,550	
Other overheads	137,400	
Capital expenditure	73,500	
Total payments		693,100
Closing cash balance		109,500

Task 4

Email

To: Production Director

From: Budget Accountant

Date: xx

Subject: Direct Labour Budget

(a)   Budget submission

I attach the proposed direct labour budget for next year for your consideration and approval.

The agreed production plan is based on a reduction in output from 450,000 units this year to 440,000 units next year.

A reduction in the time taken to produce each unit of 1% compared to the current year has been allowed for. This is an anticipated efficiency saving due to the use of some new machinery that is shortly to be installed.

An increase in the current labour rate has been incorporated into the budget. This increase of 2.2% is in line with the forecast regional labour cost index.

The total direct labour cost for next year is £278,240 based on these assumptions.

Please let me know if you need any further information.

(b)   Inherent risks

The various assumptions built into the budget could prove to be inaccurate and this would result in risks to the budget. These include:

- The budget is based on 440,000 units being produced. If this forecast is inaccurate then it will impact on the direct labour costs.

- The budget assumes that the direct labour requirement is entirely in proportion to the production level. If there is a part of the labour requirement that does not behave in this way (for example the time taken to set up production runs may form a stepped fixed cost) then the hours required may differ from the budget.

- Since the total number of direct labour hours required is fewer than this year there could be costs involved in transferring staff to other duties or even redundancy costs.

- Installation of the planned new machinery could be delayed which would reduce or eliminate the expected efficiency saving of 1%. If the machinery is installed on time the efficiency saving may not be as expected.

- The wage rate increase is based on the expected rise in the regional labour cost index. This index may prove an unreliable estimate of the costs that this company incurs, which will depend on the company wage negotiations which have not yet concluded.

Task 5

(a)

Descriptions	Term	
The result of budget data based on over-estimation of costs or under-estimation of income	Goal congruence	
	Budgetary slack	✔
	Performance related pay	
	Feedforward	
The imposition of budgets by senior managers without the participation of operational budget holders	Participative budgeting	
	Bottom-up budgeting	
	Top-down budgeting	✔
	Activity based budgeting	

(b)

	Budget for the year	Budget for June
Units sold	144,000	12,500
Units produced	150,000	13,000
	£	£
Sales	792,000	68,750
Cost of production:		
Materials used	405,000	35,100
Labour	220,000	18,900
Variable production overhead	15,000	1,300
Fixed production overhead	24,000	2,000

(c)

Draft operating budget	First Draft	Revision
Sales units	120,000	144,000
	£	£
Sales price	15.00	13.50
Sales revenue	1,800,000	1,944,000
Variable production costs	1,320,000	1,584,000
Fixed production costs	130,000	130,000
Gross profit	350,000	230,000
(Decrease) in gross profit		(120,000)

Task 6

(a)

Description	Term	
The standard cost variance that records the difference between the flexed direct labour budget and the actual cost of direct labour	Total direct cost variance	
	Direct labour rate variance	
	Direct labour cost variance	✔
	Direct material efficiency variance	

(b)

Direct raw material costs		Fav / Adv
Flexed budget (standard cost)	£56,448	
Actual price per kilo (to £0.01)	£3.62	
Actual material used per item	1.63 kg	
Price variance (to nearest £)	£344	Adv
Usage variance (to nearest £)	£1,058	Adv
Cost variance	£1,402	Adv
Cost variance % (to 0.01%)	2.48%	

(c)

Direct labour cost statement	£
Standard labour cost of production	165,900
Labour rate variance	2,100
Labour efficiency variance	−2,100
Labour cost variance	0

Task 7

Reporting results

	Flexed budget	Actual	Variances
	£	£	£
Sales revenue (60,000 units)	1,740,000	1,710,000	−30,000
Costs:			
Materials	660,000	650,000	10,000
Labour	390,000	404,000	−14,000
Distribution	228,000	248,000	−20,000
Energy	102,000	117,000	−15,000
Equipment hire	45,000	55,000	−10,000
Depreciation	25,000	26,000	−1,000
Marketing	70,000	69,000	1,000
Administration	45,000	44,000	1,000
Total costs	1,565,000	1,613,000	−48,000
Operating profit	175,000	97,000	−78,000

Task 8

Reasons for Variances

The sales volume was lower than the original budget planned, with sales at 2,000 units instead of the expected 2,500 units. The budget has been flexed to the actual level of 2,000 units and variances calculated accordingly.

The revenue variance reveals a price increase from the budgeted £45 per unit to an average £47 per unit. This resulted in a favourable variance of £4,000. There may be a link between the increased price and the volume reduction from first budgeted, and there could also be a link with the reduced advertising noted below.

The materials used were in line with expectations for the revised volume, so the adverse variance of £3,000 must be due to an average buying price of £7.50 per unit compared with the budgeted £6 per unit. This needs to be investigated.

The reduced level of output created some idle time amongst the labour force. This increased the labour cost per unit to £9.50 from the budgeted £9.00 despite the wage rate being as planned.

There was a change in power supplier which resulted in reduced power costs overall. Although the variable cost of power increased from £5 to £6.50 per unit produced, the new supplier does not impose a fixed charge. This resulted in an overall favourable power variance of £2,000.

The depreciation charge for the year was adjusted upwards to account for a review of non-current asset lives in which the estimated remaining useful lives of some assets were reduced. This resulted in an adverse variance of £600.

The planned advertising campaign was scaled back and this saving resulted in a favourable variance of £4,000. However, in combination with the selling price increase, this may have contributed to the reduction in sales volume. An analysis of this area should be undertaken to establish the most profitable policy.

The administration costs were in line with the budget.

Overall the operating profit was £2,900 greater than the flexed budget showed, since the favourable variances related to sales revenue, power and marketing outweighed the various adverse variances.